Happy Moth...

lots of ...

Andrew

Joseph

and

Pauline
xxx

A Mother's Book
of Prayer

Kevin
Mayhew

First published in Great Britain in 1994 by
KEVIN MAYHEW LTD
Rattlesden
Bury St Edmunds
Suffolk IP30 0SZ

ISBN 0 86209 541 7

Printed in Hong Kong
by Colorcraft

Contents

F. Hippolyte-Lucas

4

Mary's Slumber Song

O child of hope, what shadows fall
across your sleeping eyes:
shadows of a future
marked by love and sacrifice?
O child of promise,
such a cost, but such a prize!
O softly slumber,
child of grace!

Child of sorrow, child of joy,
child of mystery divine,
may your peaceful, trusting sleep
be of hope the seal and sign.
O softly slumber,
child of grace!

Michael Forster

WHEN YOU'RE LONELY

When you're lonely,
I wish you love.

When you're down,
I wish you joy.

When you're troubled,
I wish you peace.

When things are complicated,
I wish you simple beauty.

When things look empty,
I wish you hope.

Everyone who loves is a child of God, and
knows God.

6

EVERYTHING IS POSSIBLE

This is impossible
for a human being,
but for God
everything is possible.

MATTHEW 19:26

LIFE'S LESSONS

After a while
you learn the difference
between holding a hand
and chaining a soul.
You learn that love isn't leaning,
but lending support.
You begin to accept your defeats
with the grace of an adult,
not the grief of a child.

You decide to build
your roads on today,
for tomorrow's ground
is too uncertain.
You help someone plant a garden
instead of waiting
for someone to bring you flowers.
You learn that God has given you
the strength to endure,
and that you really do have worth.

SOLOMON'S WISDOM

God, you gave me a child,
originally part of me,
initially dependent on me,
given to me to love,
to nurture,
and to set free.

Not mine to possess,
but mine to love;
not mine to own,
but mine to respect;
not mine to grasp at,
but mine to hold.

God give me Solomon's wisdom,
to recognise true love
in the willingness to let go.

MICHAEL FORSTER

Lord, you have given
so much to me.
Give one thing more:
a grateful heart.

The fruit of the Spirit is love,
joy, peace, gentleness, goodness,
faith, meekness, temperance.

GALATIANS 5:22-23

GROWING UP

How difficult it seems
to watch our children grow up!
They start to think for themselves,
make their own mistakes,
as well as repeating ours.
Sometimes, we don't understand them.
Sometimes, they don't understand us.
They bring us pain,
they bring us joy.
Either way, we want to cling,
keep them close to us.

Mary watched Jesus grow up,
heard things she didn't understand,
saw things she didn't like,
felt things she'd have liked to avoid.
Sometimes, she thought he was crazy.
Sometimes, he thought she was slow.
But when he needed her,
she was there for him,
not that she could *do* anything,
except be there.

That's the hard part.
That's when it's *really* difficult
to watch our children grow up!

MICHAEL FORSTER

A FAMILY PRAYER

Lord, bless our family
with openness,
with sharing in all
our joys and sorrows,
with freedom to let
each other grow,
with understanding
and with love,
no matter what,
no matter where.

Every work of love
brings a person
face to face
with God.

MOTHER TERESA

GOD, OUR FATHER AND MOTHER

God, we call you 'Father',
for so we have been taught.
May we also call you 'Mother'?
You who, out of your own Being,
brought creation to birth;
you who, in love and joy,
conceive and nurture life;
you who, in hope and agony,
offer it to creation?
May we not call you Mother?

And if we do, what then?
May we not find our experiences,
our hope and dreams,
our pain and vulnerability,
our strength, our courage,
our commitment to life,
our joy and fulfilment
in you?

You know us.
You know our experiences,
you own our pain,
you share our gladness.
We love you as our Father,
and it is our joy to call you Mother.

MICHAEL FORSTER

19

Love is patient and kind;
it is not jealous or conceited or proud;
Love is not ill-mannered
or selfish or irritable;
Love does not keep a record of wrongs;
Love is not happy with evil

but is happy with the truth.
Love never gives up;
and its faith, hope and patience
never fail.

I Corinthians 13:4-7

Jesus' parents were astonished
to see him in the temple.
'What are your doing here?'
his mother asked him,
'Didn't you know we'd be worried?'
'Why were you worried?' he asked,
'Didn't you know I must be
about my Father's business?'

LUKE 2:48-49

Seeing his mother,
with the beloved disciple,
standing near the cross,
Jesus said to her,
'Mother, there is your son.'
Then he said to the disciple,
'Son, there is your mother.'
And the disciple took her
into his own home.

JOHN 19:25-27

GOD HAS NOT PROMISED

God has not promised
sun without rain,
joy without sorrow,
peace without pain.
But God has promised
strength for the day,
rest for the labour,
light for the way,
grace for the trials,
help from above,
unfailing sympathy,
undying love.

I love you
with an everlasting love.

JEREMIAH 31:3

25

It was I who taught
Ephraim to walk,
I took them up in my arms;
but they did not know
that I healed them.
I led them with cords
of human kindness,
with bands of love.
I was to them like those
who lift infants to their cheeks.
I bent down to them and fed them.

HOSEA 11:3-4

Eve said, 'With God's help, I have brought a
child into being.'

GENESIS 4:1

THE MOTHERHOOD OF GOD

Mother eternal,
making and mending,
taking and tending
all whom you bear;
gladly you love us,
sadly reprove us,
nothing can move us
out of your care.

Love full of beauty
showing and sharing,
cradling and caring
in your embrace;
each of us knowing,
tenderness showing,
watching us growing,
giving us space.

Maker maternal,
touching and tending,
seeking and sending,

fill us with grace;
stir and amaze us,
chide us and praise us,
lovingly raise us
up to your face.

MICHAEL FORSTER

A Blessing

May the Lord bless you
and take care of you;

May the Lord be kind
and gracious to you;

May the Lord look on you with favour
and give you peace.

Numbers 6:22-27

ACKNOWLEDGEMENTS

The publishers wish to express their gratitude to Fine Art Photographic Library, London and the Galleries listed below for permission to reproduce the pictures in this publication:

Front cover STILL LIFE OF CARNATIONS by Leo Louppe (b.1869).
Mark Hancock Gallery.

Page 4 STILL LIFE OF SUMMER FLOWERS AND FRUIT by Marie Felix Lucas Hippolyte.
Mark Hancock Gallery.

Page 7 A SUMMER'S DAY by James MacKay (fl.1880-1904).
Anthony Mitchell Fine Paintings, Nottingham.

Page 8 A STILL LIFE OF YELLOW ROSES WITH LILAC by Raoul de Longpre.
Fine Art of Oakham.

Page 11 SUMMER'S DELIGHT by Hermann Seeger (b.1857).
Anthony Mitchell Fine Paintings, Nottingham.

Pages 12 & 13 SPRINGTIME by Christian Zacho (1843-1913).

Page 15 THE BULLFINCH by Marcus Stone (1840-1921).
Apollo Gallery.

Page 16 THE GRAPE HARVEST by Eugen Johann Georg Klimsch (1839-1896).
Anthony Mitchell Fine Paintings, Nottingham.

Page 19 BASKETS OF STRAWBERRIES, RASPBERRIES AND CONVOLVULUS by Eloise Harriet Stannard (fl.1852-1893). Burlington Paintings.

Pages 20 & 21 PICKING BUTTERCUPS by Helen Allingham (1848-1926).
Bourne Gallery.

Page 22 EVESHAM VILLAGE by Arthur Claude Strachan (1865-1954).
City Wall Gallery.

Page 25 THE MILL MEADOW, SEFTON by Thomas MacKay (fl.1893-1916).
Bourne Gallery.

Page 26 CERNAES BAY, NORTH WALES by Noel Smith.
St Peter's Fine Art.

Page 29 A SPRING HEDGEROW WITH PANSIES AND BUTTERFLIES by George Goodman (fl.1860-1868). Private collection.

Page 30 A DOE WITH HER FAWN by Samuel John Carter (1835-1892).
Mark Hancock Gallery.